This edition published by Burning Eye Books 2014

www.burningeye.co.uk

@burningeye

Burning Eye Books

15 West Hill, Portishead, BS20 6LG

ISBN 978 1 90913 645 8

A.F. Harrold is an English po performs for adults and childre and in basements, in fields a Festival Website's Poet-in-Resid in-Residence at Cheltenham Li the Cheltenham All-Stars Slam (work broadcast on BBC Radio 4, Radio 3 and BBC 7. He is active in schools work, running workshops, showing off and doing poem-stuff at ungodly hours of the morning, and has published several previous collections of poetry. He is the owner of many books, a handful of hats, a few good ideas and one beard. He is also the author of a number of Bloomsbury-published children's novels including the quite funny *Fizzlebert Stump* series.

Lies My Mother Never Told Me

A.F. Harrold

Burning Eye

For Kate Paice, Sarah Horne & Emily Gravett –
three fine collaborators (but not on this book)

Contents

The Fashionable Gherkin

Optional Appendix – Catricide

Section One

Lies My Mother
Never Told Me

My Mother

My mother
always encouraged me to talk
to strangers.

'You never know,'
she said,
'when one of them might have some sweets.'

Gifts

As a child I was always clean-shaven,
as unsurprisingly smooth-cheeked
as all my pre-pubescent peers,
and no one guessed,
no one placed bets
on what the years would bring,
in spite of Mr Gillette
and Mr Bic's best efforts:
the lovely grown-up bearded me.

But they should've known,
should've had the inkling of an insight
when they saw,
bent over the rim of my crib,
bestowing gifts with a waggle of her wand,
the pink-frocked, beautiful, plump sight
of my very own,
uninvited, delightful, magic-wish-granting,
blessing-bestowing
Furry Godmother.

Listening to the Grateful Dead

I listen to the Grateful Dead
lying side by side with Fred.
We do not touch, we do not speak,
we do it several times a week.

Sometimes we lie on our bed
and sometimes on the floor instead.
We do not hum, it's not allowed,
though sometimes we invite a crowd.

We take with us a loaf of bread
to ensure we are both well fed.
It's said that people spend their time
in different ways. This is mine.

I listen to the Grateful Dead
in London, Stroud and Maidenhead.
I'm very pleased to have a hobby.
I learnt it from Fred's brother Bobby.

Making an Exhibition of Myself

I went to the Ideal Mirror Exhibition
at the London Olympia just last week.

Didn't see any mirrors there.

Lots of pictures of me, though.

Seemed a bit odd.

Glasses

I went for one of those
free eye-tests at the optimist's the other day.

He said things were looking up.

Lies My Mother Never Told Me

She never explained how dogs
are just cats in dog suits,

or how elephants are marionettes
controlled by clouds.

She never taught me that ants
can only count to seven,

or that birds are unique
and accidental flying assemblages of dust.

She never told me many things.
For instance, about jam:

how finding a ladybird in jam
means it's going to rain;

how finding a horse in jam
means your luck's about to change.

She never had me believe
north migrates south for the winter,

or that splinters
are a tree's preferred mode of reproduction.

She never made me make a wish
when I saw a pavement,

or a postman,
or a cat dressed in a dog suit.

I wish she'd told me more lies,
set the world spinning like a brick

poised between falling and flying,
distracted in that stomach moment,

butterflies weightless and still
before the humpback bridge

lurches them back to life,
believing moles build mountains, slowly,

believing rock strata's a decoration
for a world in need of cheering up.

Not Fair

The first 'F' fell off the *Funfair* sign, again.

Everyone began shoving on the dodgems,

no one but stallholders won cuddly toys
and gullible little goldfish in plastic sacks,

and the Hall of Magic Mirrors
made everybody look fat,
even people who were actually fat already.

In the Tunnel of Love
all the action was happening
in the car in front of mine,

as my girlfriend pointed out
on her mobile phone
from the car in front.

Poem Too Sweet

I love the shape of you
the neck and nape of you

the scrape of you
the moist pop of the grape of you

the underpants
the quiff and cape of you

I love the uncharted song of you
the tall and thin and long of you

crowd me: I'll admit I love the throng of you
leave me: I love the *where've you gone?* of you

I love the inner leg measurement of you
the loose-cannon unelected parliament of you

the discarded slag-heap slump of you
the goods-yard whistle, rattle and thump of you

I love the shunt of you
the back, side, top, bottom and front of you

the fallen off the back of a lorry and going cheap of you
the taking pleasure in making small children weep of you

the misunderstanding the correct way to pluralise the word
'sheep' of you
I love the whole heap of you

it's strange how quickly I found
I love the sky and ground of you

the spring is all around of you
the thawing dripping sound of you

when ill I love the flu of you
I sail the ship: I joined the crew of you

one day I shook hands with the *how do you do?* of you
and now I suppose it's true I love the you of you

With You

You're all I'll ever need, you're the Morecambe to my Wise,
you're the Pete to my Dud, the Derek to my Clive.

You're the Ronnie to my Ronnie, the Sitwell to my snob,
the Bert to my Ernie, the Bing to my Bob.

You're the French to my Saunders, the Marmite to my toast,
you're the mould in my cheese, you're the crabs on my coast.

You're the bag in my teapot, you're the jerk to my goat,
you're the mash to my sausage, the gravy in my boat.

You're the rustle to my parcel, you're the lick of my stamp,
you're the silk in my coffin, you're the smell of my tramp.

The Box Song

If I were a box
I wouldn't have a lid;
give me all your treasures
but don't expect them hid.

If I were a box
I'd be *fairly* robust;
my corners would be suitable
for storing fluff and dust.

If I were a box
I'd be made of wood;
not the top-notch sort of stuff,
but something not so good,
like balsa or splinters
all glued up together,
which might light a fire
but which won't keep out weather
when it's snowy or rainy
or stormy or such.
If I were a box
I'd not be good for much.

If I were a box
I wouldn't have a lock;
the review in *Which?* magazine
would simply say *What?*

The Decrepitude of the Poet

I've got athlete's foot.
I've got miner's lung.
I've got cauliflower ear
and carpenter's thumb.

I've got housemaid's knee.
I've got rising damp.
I've got writer's block
and writer's cramp.

I've got taxman's twitch.
I've got librarian's eye.
I've got poker face
and spinster's sigh.

I've got tennis elbow.
I've got sousaphone pout.
I've got trumpeter's cheek
and port-drinker's gout.

I've got golfer's grip.
I've got jogger's nipple.
I've got OAP's hip
and footballer's dribble.

I've got policeman's truncheon.
I've got burglar's stoop.
I've got wino's nose
and brewer's droop.

I've got bishop's finger.
I've got acrobat's back.
I've got juggler's balls
and postman's sack.

The Mortal Zodiac

Leo: a day at the zoo can rarely be beaten,
unless you're the one that the lion's just eaten.

Virgo: midway through his first fuck –
heart attack – out of luck.

Libra: the kitchen scales weigh and count –
arsenic has no safe amount.

Scorpio: the jungle is full of marvellous fruits –
but guess who forgot to first look in his boots.

Sagittarius: raise your shields when the arrows fly –
or like Harold look up for a sign in the sky.

Capricorn: the kid just won't stop butting in –
the impatient troll turns gruff, then grim.

Aquarius: down in the wet stuff – tries to breathe –
doesn't quite manage it – time to leave.

Pisces: eating his dinner – dining alone –
swallows a fish – chokes on a bone.

Aries: down on the farmyard – look at all the sheep –
the one with the horns is also made of meat.

Taurus: the difference between a bull and a cow?
Trip up in Pamplona – worked it out now?

Gemini: shoot one twin through the head –
empathically linked – both drop dead.

Cancer: makes you sick – makes you thin –
the bugger does what it says on the tin.

Spirals

I keep the kingfisher
on a perch
above the sink.

He likes the rippling water,
the splash of my hands
shifting crockery.

When washing the fish
I move him
to the bathroom,

where he watches
the water flow from the basin,
clockwise, I think.

Once we went
to Australia.
Things were different there.

Dave

Thursday.
A man knocked at the door,
asked if Dave was home.

I said, 'I don't know.
Where does he live?
I'll go and check for you.'

The man apologised,
said he had got the wrong house.
Went to his car. Drove away.

Friday came.
He didn't knock again.
That was our one and only meeting.

But, like Robert Plant, it made me wonder.
Now, whenever I pass a house with a door,
I have to stop myself knocking.

Does Dave live there?
Is he home?
Who's Dave?

I Like You Like a Simile Likes to Be Like Something

You're like pine-fresh scented aspirin,
like extravagant cement,
like a high-priority penguin,
while I'm just an ordinary gent.

You're like an enigmatic biscuit,
like a bubbly disco book,
like a patriotic milkshake,
and I'm only having a look.

You're like a handy self-heating hot-dog,
like some vibrant vibrating shampoo,
like a set of atomic dentures.
I'm not sure I'm worthy of you.

You're like a mentholated life-raft,
like a quiet inflatable beer,
like an obedient homing bikini.
If you need me I'll be over here.

You're like an addictive gazebo,
like a self-cleaning waterproof cat,
like a decaffeinated obelisk.
Don't panic, I'm getting my hat.

My Maiden Plant

My pot plant's the only virgin in the flat;
she's shy and always blushes tenderly
when people mention the bumblebee.

Accidental Poem

It's fallen from my trouser
    and it's crawled across the floor.
I'm feeling so embarrassed
    I just can't say any more.

A Few Lines on Stillness

When making love, surely,
the spectacular event is not,
as proposed in cliché,
the Earth moving
(it can't help but move –
the attraction of gravitational laws
sees to the continuousness of that).

Instead, surely,
the spectacular event would be,
must be, when the Earth stops –
when everything ceases to spin,
to hurtle, to bustle,
and is surprised into heartless stillness
for even the minutest of moments –

oh, then, surely,
something special,
something unutterably special
will have happened
and a blackbird falls silent,
a blue whale begins a new song –

and then the world picks up again,
almost exactly where it left off.

Small Ad

Poet needs new muse.
Looks unimportant.
Poet not too choose-
y, or too good.
Please reply by Tues-
day, if you would.

The Literary Relic Poem

Like many folk in our profession I'm fond of literary history;
I mean the stories and lives of writers mean a lot to me
and I'm a bit of an anorak.
I've bought a bit of this and that from auctions and whathaveyou,
for example the odd piece of William Makepeace Thackeray knick-
    knackeray,
if you see what I mean,
and when I'm stuck for inspiration I'll take out some object,
some relic I've collected, and I'll just hold it for a bit
(and maybe give it a little stroking)
and sometimes, and really I'm not joking,
sometimes I'll get an idea or two,
and I like to think the previous owner's essence is (sort of) coming
    through.
Anyway, that's enough of the mystical preamble.
I know people like you only visit me with the expectation
of a little inspection of the literary relics in my collection, so here
    we go…

Here in my study look to the glass cabinets on the wall
and there, underneath a rare authenticated Wordsworth
    manuscript
which has, to be fair, been knocked about a bit,
down at the bottom,
now looking slightly rotten,
are Aphra Behn's pens.
Above them is Dorothy Parker's Parker,
William Gibson's nibs and papers,
and looking better leant across Beatrix Potter's jotter's
Pablo Neruda's ruler,
which he used to underline important words
on Somerset Maugham's forms
and James Joyce's invoices.

On the other side of my study,
securely tucked away

in what was once Leo Tolstoy's tallboy,
you'll find the only extant fragment of one of Kafka's kaftans
(alongside Sartre's garters,
Mary Shelley's wellies,
Walter de la Mare's flowery flares,
Brian Patten's satin hat and
Hilaire Belloc's smocks, socks
and various frocks belonging to the Brontës).

Leaving my study and moving into the hall you'll see,
draped across one of Baudelaire's favourite chairs,
John Ruskin's buskins
beside Mervyn Peake's peaked cap that
might be made from a bite of material from Keats's kite.
And there, stood upright in Samuel Beckett's bucket
is what I assume's Sassoon's bassoon
(although to be fair the provenance of that is rather unclear).

Moving from here
into the kitchen you'll see some of my favourite prizes.
In that cupboard there is Dame Iris Murdoch's dandelion and
    burdock,
Philip Larkin's parkin, Graham Greene's beans,
John Milton's Stilton, John Donne's buns,
Les Murray's curries, Tennyson's venison,
William Blake's various cakes,
and Kipling's various cakes.
Edward Albee and Harper Lee both donated their tea to me,
and I keep it in one of Thomas Mann's cans.
On the side there is Robert Graves' microwave,
in this drawer I keep Ivor Cutler's cutlery,
that one's got Richard Dawkins' fork in,
the tall jar houses Christina Rossetti's spaghetti,
and there, in Samuel Taylor Coleridge's new and old fridges,
are Anthony Trollope's scallops
and Dr Seuss's juices, respectively.

At this point someone usually asks me where the alcohol is,
but of course that's in the sitting-room drinks cabinet.
In there I have Saki's sake, Germaine Greer's beers,
Edward Lear's beers, Ray Mears' beers,
Patricia Beer's beers, Shakespeare's beers,
Einstein's fine wines and Italo Calvino's vino.

Stepping into the bathroom you can find
the mirror used for scowling by J.K. Rowling,
a wide selection of Allen Ginsberg's chin fur,
a number of Alexander Pope's soaps,
Frank O'Hara's mascara,
an ointment made from Conan Doyle's boils,
the noisome lingering unholy stench of H.P. Lovecraft's bubble
    bath,
some recordings of Roger McGough's coughs and Alan Moore's
    snores,
a candid photo taken when Noël Coward showered,
some tissues from when Camus caught flu,
and, although I missed out the first time,
I did get a hanky from when Spike Milligan fell ill again.

Heading toward my bedroom, I'll direct your gaze out this window
into the kitchen garden below.
Pecking the ground beside Kurt Vonnegut's water butt
are Emily Dickinson's chickens and,
just to show how broadminded I am, that waddling beauty there
is John Updike's dyke duck.

(On the windowsill, in case you're bored,
are Arthur Rimbaud's dominoes. No?)

Okay, this is the bedroom, the lighting's dim
but the relics are well worth a squint.
In this case here you'll see Philip K. Dick's dick,
Michael Moorcock's cock, Stephen King's thing,

and Ezra Pound's pound of meat.
And in case you think that that's hard to beat,
in this case I've got Dylan, Edward and R.S. Thomas's
John Thomases, Edwin Morgan's organ
and Simon Schama's charmer.
The third case houses Thom Gunn's gun,
Pasternak's knick-knack, Louis MacNeice's piece,
René Descartes' part, Neil Gaiman's stamen
and, my favourite, Henry Wadsworth's Longfellow itself.

On the shelf up above is Émile Zola's old tombola
but we're not having a raffle draw tonight, I'm afraid,
so pop your tickets away; the tour's over and it's time to go home.

Thanks for coming;
it's always a treat to meet fellow literary enthusiasts.

Now, when reversing out of the car park
do be careful not to dent J.G. Ballard's bollard,
or to knock into W.H. Auden's cordon,
and here, take this with you, for the journey;
it's a complimentary copy of the original Margaret Drabble Travel
    Scrabble.

Section Two

As the Actress Said

Abigail

The policeman called on Abigail's parents
shortly after her eighth birthday.

He explained how they'd had several complaints
from men walking in the vicinity of Abigail's school

who had each been approached by a little girl
matching her description

who had demanded that they share their sweets,
even though they'd bought them for their own personal
        enjoyment.

If they had planned on sharing them, they said,
they would've bought more in the first place.

Worse than this, however,
was the policeman's next report.

One gentleman had been driving home
from the nearby pedigree pet shop

with a precious litter of pedigree puppies
when a little girl climbed into his car

and demanded, in no uncertain terms,
to look at his recently acquired pets.

Naturally he had tried to be polite,
explaining that the lights were about to change

and that he rather wanted to drive off, homewards,
but also that the puppies were awfully shy,

being so young, and that they should be left
in peace for the moment. Please.

When Abigail had pressed her hand on his knee,
smiled big cow eyes and whined,

'Oh please, sir, just a little peek and one quick stroke,'
the gentleman attempted to escape

and was knocked down by a passing ice-cream van.
The pedigree puppies were unharmed.

The policeman asked Abigail's parents if they,
maybe, couldn't control their daughter better,

and they considered cancelling her assertiveness classes.
If she would let them.

The Question of Cardboard Boxes

'Mummy?' Edwina asked her mother.
'Where did cats live
before there were cardboard boxes?'

She chewed the inside of her cheek
thoughtfully,
even though they'd just had lunch,
three hours previously.

'I don't know,' her mother answered.

She had to admit, the question *was* intriguing.
It was what her father would have called
'an intriguing question'.

They went to the library
and looked it up in books.

Passing a dense paragraph
of difficult prose
through the machinery of her brain,
Edwina's mother began to explain,
'There *were* no cats before cardboard boxes,
Edwina, my dear.
The cardboard boxes
are the ones the cats were delivered in.'

'Is it convergent evolution?'
Edwina asked.

'Possibly, possibly,'
her mother remarked,
wondering where they should go for tea.

Birdlife

Impressed
by their singing,
their feathers
and their flying,
Simon climbed
his garden's tree
and built a nest
in the branches.

He gobbled worms
and sang joyously
at the sun's rising.

He flew arms out
with enthusiastic
amounts of flapping.

Nevertheless
featherless he fell
and, caught by the cat,
that was that.

Geometries of Love

Simon dreams of Suzi in the darkness of the night,
underneath the duvet in his sleep he holds her tight,

but Suzi dreams of Peter, the peach within her eyes,
and late at night in somnolence her hand ascends his thighs,

but Peter's hugging Simon in the snugness of his dreams,
though when you're watching closer this isn't all it seems –

he thinks that Simon's frozen, that he's ice down to the core,
and Peter's hoping, maybe, that this will help him thaw.

Uncle Frank

Uncle Frank
often drank
and drew a blank
in the morning.

Let this be a warning.

Aunt Jemima

Aunt Jemima
was never finer
than on the liner
in all her jewellery and her swank.

She caught this snobbish ballroom mania
on the *Lusitania*

and then it sank.

A Sailor's Life Isn't All Plain Sailing

Sometimes in the Navy it happens
that desperate situations arise
and desperate choices must be made
and usually then it's an able seaman who gets eaten.

So, having a fine sense of duty
and knowing his place
as a plank in the flank of the larger entity
that the Royal Navy is and always must be,
Frank wouldn't normally have complained,

but since, on the day he woke up
to the smell of salt and the squawk of gulls
to discover that the captain
had started eating him,
he was in his bunk
in his cabin
in port,
he did feel some questions needed raising.

A Shellfish Poem

Kevin,
a barnacle,
clung
to the underside
of the ship
like a limpet.

The limpets
took offence
at his impression
and just let go,
drifting into the deep
like hard-edged snow.

Down below
octopi
put on hard hats
and prepared
to eat well.

Rotten Uncle Ringo

Uncle Ringo
and his dingo
went to bingo halls

and stole the balls.

Uncle Quentin

It was for his vasectomy
that Uncle Quentin
went in.

But due to unfortunate cuts
in the hospital
he lost it all.

The Mouse Story

Simon was hunting in the Forest of Dean
when he shot a mouse.

Everyone said what a brilliant shot it must have been,
because a mouse is very small
and often quite a long way away.

What no one knew at the time, though,
was that it was actually Simon's pet mouse
that he had trained years before to catch bullets in its teeth
and to play dead.

Eventually, though, the truth came out
when the mouse wrote its autobiography –
For the Love of Cheese –
in which it listed every con trick it had ever been involved in.

Simon was shocked.

Most of the revelations were simple cheese insurance scams,
but there,
in the section of colour plates near the middle of the book,
was Simon's photograph,
shot quite badly and from a very low angle,
with a caption underneath that read:
This man made me do things that really went against my morals,
but boy did he give good cheese.

As a consequence
his Forest of Dean League of Special Hunters' Sharpshooter Trophy
was repossessed,
and although no one talks to him at the club any more,
sometimes he gets the feeling
that behind his back they're still squeaking about him.

Alternative Therapy

She's old-school –

trained in the ways of doctoring
pre-penicillin, blood tests and inflatable splints.
She's a strict doctor of the mothering kind.

To her mind, you'd find,
there is no wound, ailment or ill,
no graze, headache, fever or flu
that can't be simply kissed better.

She loves her patients
and has the patience to love.

Although she also has a certain amount of good sense
and always avoids
haemorrhoids.

Disillusioned Yuppie

He thought he'd feel special
with his off-shore bank account.

But in actual fact
having to always use
the cash point at the far end of the pier
began to become
a bit of a drag.

Threesome

When he asked his wife
for a *ménage à trois*
for his birthday
she, being a little hard of hearing,
bought him
a particularly crap zoo.

Pizza Story

On top of her pizza
Jessica liked to have
tomato sauce,
basil, mushrooms,
chopped tomatoes,
various cheeses
and another pizza,
mirrored, inverted,
lidding the thing.

Disapprovingly
her mother indulged her
until the day Jessica
made a loud complaint,
flung her plate to the floor,
skittering sauce
across the linoleum,
appalled at the fact
her mother had
served it upside down.

Jessica's mother
decided enough was enough
and put Jessica up for adoption,
a tricky sell
considering the girl was twenty-seven,
married to Steven
and was adopted already.

As the Actress Said

Once upon a time there was an actress
who was acting in a stage play
off-off-Broadway
and her mother happened along to the theatre
one night,
took fright
and flight
and sent her husband instead the next night.

The father of the actress
looked at his daughter in the first scene of the play
and felt uncomfortable with her undressedness
and so, kindly, hurried onto the stage
to lend her his coat.
Now this rocked the boat
and the actor
who acted
on stage with the actress
found improvisational challenges difficult and fled.
The father asked,
'Was it something I said?'
to his daughter, the actress, not lying nude on the bed
any more
on the stage,
who was (to be honest) entering into the tiniest rage.

She spoke curtly and shortly
to her father
who'd rather, he said, that she'd not take that tone
or else wait till they're home
and alone.

The actress replied that the stage was her home
and her body was art,
or at least in this part,
and she only displayed

what he and his good wife had made
and to people who'd paid.

'I've one thing to say,' he said,
sitting down on the edge of the foot of the bed.
'Neither your mother nor I is a prude;
in fact it is true
we spend quite a bit of our time in the nude
(although I'll admit when preparing hot food
an apron is handy (especially when frying)),
but striding round naked up here on this stage
with your actor friend drying up with each line
with either his bad or his no sense of time
is not any way for a daughter of mine
to be spending her time.

'And futhermore,' he went on,
'this is a show with no songs
and the theatre's so draughty
and the script is so thin,
it's not the right play for you to be in.
A daughter like you,
who's the apple of your mother and I's eyes,
deserves so much better.'

'I don't want to be seen as a quitter,'
the daughter replied.
'An actress who leaves at the first curtain
is certain to never get work in this city again,
and then
what am I going to do
to make Mother and you
proud of me?'

'We'll always be proud...'
The rest of his sentence was drowned by the loud

roar of the crowd,
who'd been watching the scene
unfolding between
the girl and her dad
and by now they had had,
in the couple's oration,
more drama and love and coiling emotion
than they could handle.

They displayed an ovation
and roared with approval
and the management of the theatre,
instead of calling for the old man's removal,
asked if he could come back every night
to highlight the plight
and turn up the tension,
and not to mention the sense of suspension
that hung in the air.

The actress's father thought he might well agree
but only after he'd got an appropriate fee.

Uncle Jack

Uncle Jack
always sat
in the back
of the car.

He never went very far
because he had great difficulty reaching the pedals.

Uncle Billy, the Dedicated Nudist

Uncle Billy
wound a woolly
round his willy
in the chilly weather.

Auntie Heather sometimes helped.

Stuffed

Simon
was a taxidermist who,
scared of the touch of flesh,
of the coolness of fur or fleece,
restricted his business
to teddy bears, rag dolls
and other miscellaneous cuddlesome companions.

At the taxidermists' club
he was looked down upon,
mentioned infrequently in newsletters,
never nominated for awards,

but, at least
(he consoled himself),

his work always sold.

You Are What You Are

Andrew's a vegetarian centenarian centurion.
Robert's a totalitarian Aryan librarian.
Daphne's a mammalian Wagnerian Victorian lesbian.
Frank's a Rastafarian proletarian old Etonian.
Erica likes linoleum.

Violet is a bohemian Babylonian Shakespearean.
Michael meets every criterion of being an historian.
Simon's an American libertarian utopian bastion.
Roger is a Northumbrian Darwinian veterinarian.
Oscar was born by caesarean.

Geoff's a nonagenarian Trinitarian barbarian.
Verity's a humanitarian accordion custodian.
Xyxxgotn'x is a gargantuan reptilian scorpion-like alien.
Neville is a thespian doing Napoleon and *Pygmalion*.
Tracy's only wearing a turban.

Sven is a stentorian Scandinavian pedestrian.
Bruce is a gargantuan agrarian Tasmanian.
William's an egalitarian antediluvian simian champion.
Stephen's an Arthurian neo-Jungian fruitarian.
Yolanda is none of the above.

Uncle Stanley

Uncle Stanley
was so manly

that old ladies
would stop him in the street

and ask to be carried across.

Shy Uncle John

Uncle John
had always gone
by the time his turn came round.

I never found out what he did.

Or where he hid.

Health

Sebastian has a bit of a sweet tooth,
but always insists on eating a balanced diet;
he is very health-conscious like that.

Every time he eats some chocolate
he will weigh it beforehand
and counterbalance it by eating
exactly the same weight's worth of fruit
or vegetables.

And every time he eats some vegetables
or fruit, or bread, cheese, meat or dessert
he weighs that too
and counterbalances it by eating
exactly the same amount of chocolate.

Sebastian's diet doesn't keep him slim
but it does keep him happy
and if kitchen scales had feelings
then his would be overjoyed with being so useful.

Inter-Rail Poem

Lorraine
in Spain

stayed mainly
on the train.

Roll Up, Roll Up

Lucy was disappointed
by her circus visit.

The tattooed man
was shy,

the juggler,
an average potter,

and the allusionist
hardly mentioned her.

Goldilocks and the Three Wise Bears

Eventually finding that the house was unlocked,
Goldilocks decided it was only right to explore.

In the kitchen she made some food and a mess.
She rifled the sideboard and the cupboards. What fun.

Upstairs she emptied each chest of drawers,
upturned the beds and rummaged in wardrobes.

She spilt the jewellery box into her rucksack
and dabbed her wrists and neck with fine scent.

Suddenly she heard a rattling downstairs.
It sounded like the handle of the kitchen door.

With cat-like tread she slipped to the window,
opened it silently and climbed onto the ledge.

There were footsteps on the stairs, heavy ones.
As the bedroom door opened she jumped.

The flowerbed beneath her contained surprises –
first a twisted ankle, then a muddy slip and fall.

A painted gnome impaled her on his rod.
She couldn't move her legs, was losing blood.

As she looked up in the night sky a star twinkled,
straight above the house, brighter than the rest.

It was blocked by the dark head of a great bear
poking out the window she had just exited from.

It withdrew. The star twinkled at her some more.
The kitchen door rattled again. Lumping footsteps.

Around the side of the house three bears prowled.
In their paws, from clawtips, hung boxes. One each.

'We followed the star,' said the first and smallest bear.
'We have travelled far and have brought you gifts.'

The largest bear plodded over and dropped its box.
'Gold,' said the smallest bear. 'I hope you like it.

'I brought you some frankincense,' it went on.
'It's an aromatic resin.' Its box joined the other.

The third bear, a medium-sized grizzly, huffed.
'I brought you myrrh,' it said, putting its box down.

'It's another aromatic resin. We didn't discuss it.
I didn't know what else you'd be getting. Sorry.'

Just before Goldilocks passed out from blood loss
she wondered if all this perfume was a personal comment,

and whether she ought to be offended, but then
she remembered the gold and the current market price.

'Thank you,' she managed to mutter, before dying.
There was a silence in the garden as her ghost gave up.

The first and smallest bear looked at the others.
'Are you sure,' it said, 'we've followed the right star?'

The medium-sized bear looked up at the sky,
then at the dead girl, then back up at the sky.

After a moment's contemplation a conclusion came.
'Actually,' it murmured softly, 'that's a helicopter.'

The three wise bears watched as the star flew off,
the sound of distant rotors now whistling down.

'Well,' said the first bear, 'let's just thank Christ
she didn't unwrap any of the presents.'

The three bears looked down at their claws
and at their shaggy fur and remembered the great effort

they'd gone to with the Sellotape and paper,
and how long they'd spent getting the ribbons right.

'You can say that again,' the second bear murmured.

Section Three

From a Certain Point of View

Trees, I

Unweighted by conspiracies of earth
we'll watch them gain the freedom of the sky,
stand beneath their sideways shrinking shade
and wave them off to dance and drift and distance,
like green hot air balloons that have let fall
all ballast at last.

Watch them tip their leaves up to the sun,
exhale like weary jets and slowly glide,
trailing thirsting roots to graze on clouds.

Forests of them drift after the dawn,
a constant lazing westwards through the day
until, outpaced by this turning earth,
night catches up and they dip in to rest,
touch down on some barren hill to roost.

They've all held nests and watched their birds so long,
listened to each morning's burst of singing,
over ages learned to hear the sky,
to love that open space of which birds speak.

The fluttering shingle sound of leaves you hear
is not the wind, but warming pre-flight checks.

Trees, II

My heart goes out across the road,
gets caught in that oak like a balloon string
and bobs there,
doomed delightfully to follow this tree
through its migratory flights.

Picture it as I do –
whole deciduous forests upping sticks
and heading south for the winter.
In late September, early October,
herdsmen in North Africa watch the skies.

Earthbound, like them, I've watched this tree
and seen the scampered games
the squirrels play –
the seeming kiss-chase race of hide and seek
they coil around the trunk without a slip.
They call it home.

But what I wouldn't give to see their faces
when one morning they wake
and scarper out to the very tip of the finest branch
and sway and dandle,
bounce and quaver elastically,
looking down through the mile of watery air
to that far green patchwork sliding into ocean grey.

Do they remember how this happens every year,
or does the shock reset the squirrel brain?
Do they think of anything but
the secret stores of acorns left behind?

Ice Age Dream

Just as the lobster, beetle and the snake
outgrow their skins and leave them lying round,
so too this mammoth sheds its winter fur,
reaches down and there, with fingered trunk,
unzips the red-haired coat and, stepping out,
revels in the new grey nudity,

the feel of sun on skin and wind that rolls
between the legs, behind the ears and out
across this landscape puddled patchily
where glaciers have gone and left their scars,
their boulders, valleys, fjords; and now the sun
is king of all the world in endless summer.

Magpies

One for sorrow, two for joy.
Three for a girl, four for a boy.

Five for silver, six for gold.
Seven for a secret not to be told.

Eight for a stranger, nine for a friend.
Ten for beginnings, eleven an end.

Twelve for compliance, thirteen's good luck.
Fourteen for potatoes, fifteen for duck.

Sixteen for a gap year filled up with travel.
Seventeen for a sweater soon to unravel.

Eighteen for passion, nineteen for ennui.
Twenty for a medium-sized shrub, twenty-one for a tree.

Twenty-two for a doctor bearing good news.
Twenty-three for a parent who insists on sharing objectionable views
    the first time you bring home your new boyfriend or girlfriend.

Twenty-four for a journey, twenty-five for at home.
Twenty-six for the sort of hat worn by a gnome.

Twenty-seven for sunset, twenty-eight for morning.
Twenty-nine for the engagement ring you're considering pawning.

Thirty to forty for happy ever after.
Forty-one to fifty: faint echoes of laughter.

Fifty-one up, wings shadow like night,
for lock all doors and windows; Hitchcock was right.

Sir Gawain and the Green Night

Sometime in the future
when man's reached further
and set more than a foot in the sky,
when his base has spread across the face
of that old silver companion,
that poetic talisman,
that symbolic symbol symbolising serenity
and lunacy,
he'll have filled the Sea of Tranquillity
with shrubbery,
filled the lower lunar orbit with atmosphere
and up there be growing bigger veg
in weaker gravity
for cheaper meals down here,
and Sir Gawain (no relation)
will walk out in the night lit
by the reflected light of that green globe,
a green glow across the desert and seas,
across the place where the trees used to be,
and, because he never studied history,
won't know the glow of the night lit by the full moon
was once bright and white.

Two Canute Poems

i. A Poem about King Canute and His Chief Advisor

Godwin's king, in Godwin's eyes,
lost God's highest given right
to being king
by paddling.

ii. Fighting the Waves

Whereas Canute
sat mute
and ineffectual
as the water lapped all
round his feet,

the dog at the seaside
puts up more of a struggle,
as if each bite, bark or tug'll
teach the sea
a lesson,

or so the courtiers reckon.

The Inside View

There once was an ugly duckling;
its feathers were stubby and grey.

All the other ducklings, the pretty ones,
sniggered and pecked and bullied away.

They called him names like
stubby-grey-duckling and *grey-stubby-duckling*
and *you-grey-ugly-motherfuckling.*

When the ugly duckling
waddled up to the farmer in tears one day
the farmer said, 'Ignore them, ugly duckling.
It's what's on the inside that really counts.
I expect on the inside you're beautiful.'

They went to the hospital
and the ugly duckling had an endoscopy.

The endoscopist peered carefully
at the little screen
and was sick down his chinos.

Mountains

Banged awake by crashing plates
they rub their eyes,
brush away the sleep,
shake loose the sheets
and they stretch,
crack their knuckles at the heavens,
crunch their shoulders, their necks,
and yawn their million-year-long yawns.

Given a mirror
they'd not recognise themselves now,
those rugged wrinkled faces,
those weathered outlooks,
features worried away by wind and water.

No, mountains remember smooth plains,
soft curves of hills and meadows,
remember bees, butterflies and flowers,
not this cold rock and cold lichen,
remember beaches, sand, and the sea,
islands, reefs, oceans,
a whole divers landscape,
not this rock
and the stony stretch mark of a receding tree line,
not all this hardness.

Shocked by the sight
of their white-haired summits
they stand winded, panting.

It's hard to take a breath, the air's so thin.

Dreams

They sleep during the hottest part of the day,
when it's brightest
and when the curtains are at their thinnest.

They don't sleep well.
The room is stuffy. The windows are shut.
Everybody else is out at work.

They wriggle about, push the sheets away,
turn the pillow over and over
trying to find the other side.

It's no wonder, then, when night falls
and they button up their overcoats
and lace up their soft shoes

and, packed supper in hand,
climb inside our heads
and go to work,

that they make little sense.
After an anxious stifled sleepless day,
in the cool muddle of the night,

the dreams begin to yawn.
Their eyelids droop and their heads loll.
In the middle of telling one story

they sit up suddenly,
saying, 'I wasn't asleep!'
and start off down a completely different path.

Holly and the Bear

One day my friend Holly told me about a beautiful idea she had.
Maybe it had come to her in a dream; I don't know.
I decided to steal her idea and use it in a poem, *this* poem in fact.

Her idea was this: 'Wouldn't it be lovely if…'
…actually *she* said, 'How cool would it be if…'
but she's young and young people talk like that.

What she meant was: 'Wouldn't the world be lovely if…'
…and it's at this point that I thought her idea really took off…
'…if bears went into hibernation in the winter,
and came out as butterflies in the spring?'

You see?
It's such an elegant thought, such a delightful conceit
that I couldn't help but wish I'd thought of it first.
I asked her if I could steal it for a poem and she said I could,
so long as I credited her in some way. So thank you, Holly.

Of course, the idea about the pandemonium was all mine.
You see, I do have some ideas left that I didn't have to steal.
'What's a pandemonium?' I imagine Holly asking me one day,
and I'd be able to say, 'It's an endangered sort of musical
    instrument.'
And then she could write a poem about that and give me some
    credit.

But bears becoming butterflies… really, that's a fine thought.

Two Legends

i. Beowulf

Oi! He kills Grendel.
And its mother. Seasons pass.
The dragon eats him.

ii. Labour No. 5

Heracles must have hoped
to get thoroughly soaped
once he was able
to deal with the stable.

A Story Poem

Once upon a time there was something very interesting
and this very interesting thing was so fascinatingly interesting
that everyone rushed round to see it and to look at it
and to watch it and to point and stare and gossip about it.

And they formed a big crowd, full of colour and bustle,
swaying this way and that, murmuring with life,
swelling with curiosity, and I was much too polite
to push my way to the front and find out what was going on.

Aubade

Due to a quirk
of latitude,
they share
the same attitude:
when Barcelona
lightens,
Brighton
brightens.

(In actual fact
that's wrong.
They share
the same long-.)

Here, There, Everywhere

On the one hand,
buses know they're better
than trains.
Buses replace trains,
never the other way around.

On the other hand,
trains look down on buses,
waiting for engine trouble
and a level crossing
to teach them who's boss.

On the third hand,
planes look down on everyone.

Happy Ever After

There once was an ugly duckling:
it grew up to be a swan.

There once was an ugly gosling:
it grew up to be a swan, too.

The once was an ugly cygnet:
it grew up to be a golden eagle.

There once was an ugly piglet:
it grew up to be a wild boar.

There once was an ugly hippo:
it grew up to be a rhinoceros.

There once was an ugly courgette:
it grew up to be a marrow.

There once was an ugly apricot:
it grew up to be an ugli fruit.

There once was an ugly child:
it grew up to be a serial killer.

Skyscraper Triptych

When René Magritte
attempts the feat
of building his own skyscraper,
he covers the thing
from floor to ceiling
with a swath of cloud-coloured wallpaper.

Salvador Dalí
looks a right Charlie
when his skyscraper's finally built
'cause one side extends
and melts and bends
and is held in the air by a stilt.

Pablo Picasso
in downtown El Paso
hands in his skyscraper plans;
the architect looks
through Picasso's sketchbooks
and says, 'Cubism's quite an apt art-form in this situation, isn't it?'

Blue Day

The forget-me-nots remembered to bloom,
the bluebells rang round the forest,
over the white cliffs improbable birds flew.

It was a blue day.
It was a new day.
It was a Tue day.

Inexplicably,
the 's' had gone missing in the night,
not to found in the cold dawn light.

A snake went to speak and had a fright,
silently.

From a Certain Point of View

Don't judge a book by its cover.
Don't judge a cook by his broth.
Don't judge a look by its glasses.
Don't judge a window-cleaner by his cloth.

Don't judge a judge by his judging.
Don't judge a handle by its door.
Don't judge a budgie by its budging.
Don't judge the seaside by the shore.

Don't judge a gambler by his bet,
or a puppy by its vet,
or a pilot by his jet,
or a fisherman by his rod,
or net.

Don't judge a diary by its entries.
Don't judge an armchair by its legs.
Don't judge an army by its sentries.
Don't judge a haircut by its head.

Don't judge a tree by its squirrels.
Don't judge a light-bulb by its switch.
Don't judge a sunset by the squirrels either.
Don't judge a fancy-dress party by its witch.

Don't judge a sandal by its buckle,
or a mickle by its muckle,
or a trickle by its truckle,
or a chick by its chuckle,

because these things all signify very little.

Spring Is Sprung

Watch it fly
excitedly out of your hands,
explosively,
as a sudden bulb goes off,
a yellow trumpet blaring
so loud
so bright
it almost takes your eye out.

Summer Beach Scene

see the little buckets
in the hands of seashell seekers

see the seashell seller
be a minefield for careless speakers

see the ice cream
leave a stain on bulging new bikini

see the new trunks
slowly suffocate constricted weenie

see the little baby
drinking milk from nipple nozzle

see the Punch & Judy man
accidentally swallow swazzle

Desert Island Risks

Cannibalism,
tatty clothes,
sunburnt shoulders,
sunburnt nose.

No fresh water,
Oliver Reed,
having to drink
what you just peed.

Falling coconuts,
rising tide,
tropical storms
and no inside
to go into to get out of the rain.

Boats shipwreck
on submerged rocks,
aeroplanes crash,
hovercrafts pop,
you'd better off stick with the train.

Duck

A duck takes to water like off a duck's back.
A duck don't deal pills, no duck is a quack.
A duck in the hand is worth two in the sack.

A duck in the pond makes another duck ponder.
A duck is a snack for a damp anaconda.
A duck in the hand makes the heart grow fonder.

A duck's not a chooser, but it's thicker than water.
A duck's mummy is just some other duck's daughter.
A duck in the hand makes the evening grow shorter.

A duck is a pearl if the duck pond's an oyster.
A duck and a monk might converse in a cloister.
A duck in the hand makes the glove grow moister.

A duck is a cygnet that's grown up too plain.
The head of a duck is all beak and no brain.
A duck in the hand can lead to a sprain.

A duck that's unholy is a duck that will float.
The duck that can't swim is the one in the boat.
A duck in the duck-house will clean out your moat.

All ducks lead to Rome, old ducks fade away.
A duck always hears all the things you don't say.
A duck in the hand is worth two on the day.

A duck in the soup with a straw always sucks.
A penguin is just a duck in a tux.
A duck in the hand is worth the same as two slightly smaller ducks.

A duck is better a safe duck than sorry.
A duck is quite useless at driving a lorry.
A duck in the hand will not bite, do not worry.

A duck in the original is all Greek to me.
A duck that makes honey is actually a bee.
A duck in the hand just yearns to be free.

A duck that glitters ain't always a duck.
A duck in a strip club drinks beer and leers – 'Oi, love, just pluck!'
A duck in the hand, when rubbed, brings good luck.

A duck that's worth doing is worth doing well.
A duck and a witch might meet up for a spell.
A duck in the hand is the cause of this smell.

A duck that is curious can out-dead the cat.
A duck on the head is just one sort of hat.
A duck in the hand is worth two on the flat.

A red duck at night was not built in a day.
A duck with a nest-egg might show you the lay.
A duck in the hand's worth a duck in the hay.

A duck out of sight is a duck somewhere else.
This disgruntled duck's being teased by an elf.
A duck in the hand won't fill an entire warehouse all by itself.

A duck is as certain as death, ducks and taxes.
A duck in the office just fowls up the faxes.
A duck in the hand brings on anaphylaxis.

This duck once was a duckling of infinite jest;
now older and stringy this duck's past its best.
A duck in the hand... oh, you think of the rest.

A duck and an orange have an uneasy friendship.
A duck with a windy way weavingly wends it.
A duck in the hand shown a poem just ends it.

Section Four

The Fashionable Gherkin

Preliminary studies for a forthcoming novel

i. The Fashionable Gherkin

Geraldine stuttered when she spoke the names of vegetables.
Hubert looked away, not embarrassed, but dog-tired with looking *at*.

A heavy snow had fallen three years before.
Silence returned as Geraldine lay down the last carrot.

The kitchen table rested underneath an envelope as Hubert read
  aloud:
Dear Sir, and so on and so forth.

Geraldine was startled and tea dribbled into the wrong hole.
Falling and coughing she knocked Hubert's jars with her
  convulsing arm.

He carefully folded the unfortunate letter away and stood up.
Jars rolled in parabolae, spilling their contents loudly across the
  linoleum.

Previously there had been nothing of the sort.
He considered speaking harshly, but wept quietly instead.

Geraldine drifted in vinegar puddles, noting the angle of a gherkin.
Jaunty, she thought, before slipping into unconsciousness.

As she dreamt, Hubert stared sadly dismissively into the future.
Toast crunched slowly between bright crisp white teeth.

ii. Sir Philip's Letter

He looked out across the ha-ha at the mist.
It had settled with the evening into dusk.
Sir Philip had only once or twice been kissed.

His mother was one woman on that list.
She'd slipped away while he chewed on a rusk.
He looked out across the ha-ha at the mist.

He'd left the others inside playing whist.
He thought he'd caught the distant scent of musk.
Sir Philip had only once or twice been kissed.

Once was with a mahout, but that tryst
was ended by a jealous thrust of tusk.
He looked out across the ha-ha at the mist.

He clutched her latest letter in his fist.
Why did it have to be so very brusque?
Sir Philip had only once or twice been kissed.

The evening is a knife life likes to twist
into a heart that's hollowed like a husk.
He looked out across the ha-ha at the mist.
Sir Philip had only once or twice been kissed.

iii. Mable's Close Shave

Mable
was unable
to concentrate for long periods of time
until the surgeon removed the slice of lime
that had become wedged
in her prefrontal cortex
during a bar fight.

After he did so, she was all right.

iv. Francis's Bear

Francis Penderby so loved his bear.
He'd taken it to bed with him for years.
A relationship like theirs was something rare.

Called up to serve he marched around the square,
cleft from his friend, in uniform and tears.
Francis Penderby so loved that bear.

A soldier's life can often be unfair.
Just mentioning his love would earn him jeers.
A relationship like theirs was something rare.

Bullied, he played a lot of solitaire.
A sketch kept in his locket staunched his fears.
Francis Penderby so loved his bear.

At home on leave he'd rub his nose in hair,
breathe deep and feel as if he'd drunk ten beers.
A relationship like theirs was something rare.

He snuck the bear back to the barracks where
the resultant carnage ended his career.
Francis Penderby so loved that bear.
A relationship like theirs was something rare.

v. Grizelda's Prayer

Grizelda Hesperus Greenfinch
was every inch
her namesake: not the beautiful bird,
don't be absurd,
but the boat.
She didn't have a face to float
men's desires,
stoke their fires
or otherwise turn their heads.
She wasn't, in short, the sort of girl who weds.

She was the sort who quietly cries
as inside something dies
day by day and inch by inch.

Grizelda Hesperus Greenfinch
had tried every tip in the book
to look
better than she naturally did.
She hid
mysteriously behind a veil,
to no avail,
wore black
to parties, sat at the back
and smoked Gauloises cigarettes
for effect.
But no one ever came near.

Fear
of dying a spinster
drove her to York Minster
where she fell on her knees
and said, 'Please,
if there's anyone up there
spare
a thought for me.
Thirty-three

and unkissed,
unloved and unmissed.'
She was very polite, but all the same
no answer came.

This absence, however, she didn't find odd;
her face had implied from birth there was no God.

vi. Grandma's Excuse

Grandma went wrong in her youth.
Something got turned in her head.
She never quite told us the truth.

Her sisters declared her uncouth –
as girls they had shared the same bed,
yet still Grandma went wrong in her youth.

Her knickers she'd dry on the roof –
oh, the neighbourhood boys were well-fed.
But she never quite told us the truth.

She would strip at a sip of vermouth,
and make any man's wife see red.
Oh, Grandma went wrong in her youth.

As she put her feet up on a pouffe,
she just laughed at what people said.
She never quite told us the truth.

It was said she saw, by some sleuth,
something lovely in the woodshed:
thus Grandma went wrong in her youth.
But she never quite told us the truth.

vii. The Accidental Herpetologist

Geraldine paced the veranda in the grim evening light.
The silhouette of Hubert's wide wings whisked through the sky.

A nondescript scream echoed out as the summerhouse exploded.
Hubert never had got the hang of gliding.

Elsewhere a grandfather clock struck the hour dustily.
Autumn was early in coming that year.

Among seed catalogues and parasols something stirred.
Hubert's awkward hand sought the greying dimming daylight.

Geraldine had seen it all before.
She sighed slowly lovingly.

Disengaged from the accumulated apparatus, Hubert emerged.
His goggles were highly protective and so he fell in the pond.

As he drifted in duckweed he noted the crest of a newt.
Great, he thought, before lapsing into apoplexy.

As he writhed Geraldine called for the gardener.
High up the first stars were making an early display of themselves.

viii. Erica's Desperate Situation

Erica was getting desperate.
The sandwiches had run out.
The Thermos was empty.

She wasn't sleeping well.
What dreams she had were hungry.
At night she heard wolves.

The dawn light broke thinly.
It was clear Bob had died in the dark.
His body looked stringy and grey.

Still, a source of food is a source of food.
Overhead an aeroplane flew.
It did not see their gravelled *SOS*.

Bob was unpleasant to the taste.
Emotions creaked.
There wasn't quite enough to go round.

Erica wept silent tears as she chewed.
She locked eyes with Captain Pearson.
He was weeping silently too.

It was the thirty-fourth day in the maze.
The survivors were all anxious, fretful.
Hampton Court would never be the same again.

ix. Lady Palimpsest's Husbands

Lady Palimpsest was most upset.
Her new husband had recently run off
when she'd only made the slightest little threat.

The previous one had barely broken sweat
when woken by her menacing little cough.
Lady Palimpsest was most upset.

Had he not been aware her epithet
was *She who wields the poker and is boss*?
(She'd only made the slightest little threat.)

She'd married him to eradicate the debt
incurred in building her temple to Thanatos.
Lady Palimpsest was most upset.

He'd emptied out the bank before he swept
out into the dark and called the cops.
But she'd only made the *slightest* little threat.

They treated her like a common suffragette.
They took away her broken riding crops.
Lady Palimpsest was most upset.
She'd only made the slightest little threat.

x. The Tournament

'In Eastbourne, with the boxing gloves,' said Cecil excitedly.

'No, Nottingham, with a fishing rod,' corrected his sister Emily impatiently.

'I thought it was Frinton-on-Sea, with an acorn,' their father added awkwardly.

'No, no,' their mother stated dolefully, 'it's in the billiard room, just the same as it was last week.'

xi. Vera's Brief Affair

Though Vera was well aware of what she'd done,
she'd not known at first the fellow was her brother.
A lot of the affair had been quite fun.

Her face was smooth and pale beneath the sun.
She kept the turmoil bubbling undercover.
Vera was well aware of what she'd done.

She marvelled at how, out of everyone,
this chap had struck her as better than any other.
A lot of the affair had been quite fun.

At an early age she'd wanted to be a nun.
Stay virginal, take Jesus for her lover.
Oh, Vera was well aware of what she'd done.

She'd never baked, yet now she had a bun.
She blamed a lack of talking with her mother.
A lot of the affair had been quite fun.

Vera had been out and bought a gun.
Someone had to be punished, someone or other.
Vera was well aware of what she'd done,
although a lot of the affair had been quite fun.

xii. The Ambiguous Haircut

The sixth week of scheduled rain was drawing to a close.
Geraldine placed a delicate cross in her notebook.

Next door a crackling fire warmed an empty room.
Hubert dripped gently onto unfolded newspapers.

An advertisement for a novel laundry-pressing device caught his eye.
It had a typographical error which made it read humorously.

Hubert suddenly remembered he had no sense of humour.
He stopped laughing and continued to drip.

Four weeks previously his hair had been cut ambiguously.
He had hurried home, head hidden beneath a small hat.

Subsequently he wrote the barber a threatening letter.
A modest book token was sent by way of apology.

Geraldine had been delighted by her birthday present.
She placed another delicate cross in her notebook.

From the kitchen window the garden glinted like a mine.
This summer flowers had been replaced by raindrops.

Optional Appendix – Catricide

In my role as a sort of Tweeting poet-in-residence at the Cheltenham Festival of Literature in 2010 I invited people to send me the names of their pets, hoping to find in there a few poems, a few seeds of ideas. Some pet names provided the genesis of several poems in The Fashionable Gherkin, *others didn't. I collected together the best of the cat names I was sent and included them in the following poem, which was read in a small marquee to an audience of several at the festival. I received no feedback.*

AFH, October 2014

The Killing of Cats

The killing of cats is a difficult matter;
it isn't just something that happens off-hand.
Sometimes, for sure, curiosity beckons,
but equally often the thing must be planned.

Lucy was able, before she was captured,
to exorcise one dozen cats from the land.
The reason, her mother later on pleaded,
was Lucy disliked a life that was bland,

and felt (the girl, that is, not the mother)
the easiest way to add spice to the thing
was by capturing, slaughtering, eliminating
pussies. Oh, death, where's thy sting?

The sting's at the end of a long fishing rod
with steak that's been seasoned with powdered glass;
Theakston, a small dark peculiar puss-cat,
was hungry and curious and soon came to pass.

Lucy went fishing from out of her window;
while sat on her bed she would jiggle the line,
but cats are not stupid and once one had bought it
the others knew better than wasting their time

with meat that was deadly, and so she adapted
her methods by buying a small clockwork mouse
and coating the fellow with essence of nightshade
and letting it rattle around in the house.

Soon Tiptoe, a hunter with natural-born instincts,
made his big pounce with poise and with ease
and, biting down hard on the fur of the mouse-toy,
soon ceased as a property heated for fleas.

Poor Dumbledore's caught by the tail in a door,
which doesn't sound too bad until we add that
the lorry was doing Southampton to Shrewsbury;
the M40 is not a good place for a cat.

Lucy was not the best of all Buddhists
so when she met Karma she tickled his chin
and stroked round his ears and ruffled his belly
and dumped the dear puss in a big wheelie bin

just as the dustmen were cresting the corner.
Oh, Lucy was evil. Lucy loved sin.
See, Goosepeg, a beautiful gingery tom cat,
she took to the lake to see if he'd swim,

but with his legs tied and covered in breadcrumbs
Goosepeg did little: he bubbled and bobbed.
The sight was so piteous as real geese mobbed him
that even our Lucy both giggled *and* sobbed.

Then Barnaby fell, late one night, in the well
and C-Fer was found when the bell would not toll
strapped by his collar to the side of the clapper,
head cracked like a overripe piece of fruit bowl.

The less said of Moppet and Moomin and Sedgwick
the better, I guess, for the truth is unclear;
they were the cats who kept mice from the cellar
of Ye Olde King's Arms. Now there's blood in the beer.

And sweet Daisy Mittens, beloved of all children,
who kept her claws in and who purred as she played,
who mothered all fledglings that fell out of nests,
whose poses with hamsters had certainly made

the careers of several local photographers
(no calendar told a twee date without her):
she vanished one night late in December
when Lucy was seen sporting mittens of fur.

The last cat to vanish while Lucy was extant,
while Lucy was carving her way through them all,
was Tripod, a three-legged and one-eyed old fighter,
who wobbled at times but was not seen to fall

until the day came when she'd read how the Martians
were finally brought down by dear H.G. Wells,
how the tripods and heat rays were finally vanquished
by the humblest of beings, those smart single cells.

Oh! Tripod the fighter, Tripod the survivor,
who'd barracked and bullied his way to each chance,
did not stand for much when he gobbled the Go-Cat
sprinkled with anthrax with barely a glance.

Lucy was happy, Lucy was laughing,
Lucy was jolly and Lucy was smug,
Lucy was dancing and Lucy was smiling,
Lucy was too proud to think that the rug

might be about to be pulled from beneath her,
that her felinicidal romances would end.
But pussies, although they tend to be solitary,
in troubling times find the means to a friend.

So each death was noted, each disappearance,
and word had gone round as to what was the cause
and clear as clear is, just one thing was certain:
her plans *must* be ended, and at cattish claws.

So Spanky and Bastard, two neighbourhood cats,
who were all that was left of a choir of ten,
sent up a twilight mewing of urgency,
which travelled, redoubled, all the way to the pen

that trundled along at the rear of the circus
in which slept a lion, ferocious on cue;
his teeth were all rubber, his claws were all blunted,
but he heard the cats' plea and knew what to do.

Cometh the dawn light, cometh the trainer,
and out jumped the lion and bounded away,
leaving the poor man dazed and confounded
lying in chuck beef, surprise and dry hay.

Spanky and Bastard were patiently waiting.
The lion arrived and grumbled a roar.
They'd watched Lucy's window, knew she was home.
Acrobatically agile they rang at the door.

Lucy came down and found on her doorstep
the King of all Cats: a lion, no less.
She didn't know fear, she didn't know panic,
she knew opportunity, pulled from her dress

a pistol she kept both oiled and loaded
and shot at the lion as it sprang in a pounce.
The whistling bullet lodged deep in the sternum;
the lion was killed, but each single ounce

of weighted momentum carried it forward;
a pounce once begun is not easily stopped.
The corpse of the lion fell full on poor Lucy.
Pinned under the thing her fingers were cropped

by the razorish teeth of Spanky and Bastard;
they nipped off the tips, they nipped off her nose,
they spat out her ears, but enjoyed her eyeballs,
they licked at her cheeks, they bit through her clothes.

Oh! Lucy was screaming, Lucy was weeping,
Lucy was struggling but Lucy was stuck,
Lucy was bleeding and Lucy was blinded,
Lucy was dying and cursing her luck.

But Spanky and Bastard were just normal cats,
with normal-sized jaws, and normal-sized teeth,
and long before they had finished with Lucy
the trainer arrived and with him the police.

She was arrested for discharging a firearm
without a licence, and taken away
raving and screaming (as much as she could
when all that remained of her tongue just lay

on the doorstep there, in a puddle of blood
with a miniature paw-print smudged in the dirt).
She never recovered, was never released,
Spanky and Bastard had dealt too much hurt,

but frankly the dark twisted girl had it coming;
you can't murder pussies and expect to go free.
A cat will have vengeance, today or tomorrow:
don't get on their wrong side, just let them be.

Spanky and Bastard, our be-whiskered heroes,
unfortunately garnered a taste for raw meat,
specifically human, and (after a series
of fortuitous incidents in which they beat

the ambulance crew to accidents' sites)
had to be captured, destroyed and renounced,
but their memory lives on in tiny cat brains
that remember the day the pouncer got pounced.

Spanky and Bastard, Tiptoe and Karma,
Dumbledore, Goosepeg and Barnaby too,
Moppet and Moomin, C-Fer and Sedgwick,
Daisy and Theakston and Tripod: I knew

all of them dearly and take off my hat
and offer this poem to their memories –
dear pussies, dear moggies. Oh, praise be the cat!
Up there in heaven, scratching their fleas.